THE
JOURNEY
OF THE
SPIRIT
OF THE
RED MAN

A MESSAGE FROM THE ELDERS

Written at the Turtle Lodge By:

Harry Bone, Sherry Copenace, Dave Courchene, William Easter, Robert Greene & Henry Skywater

With Contributions from Peter Atkinson & D'Arcy Linklater

Featuring Original Paintings by Henry Guimond

Order this book online at www.trafford.com
or email orders@trafford.com or email orders@traff ord.com.
To order this book directly from the authors,
order this book online at http://theturtlelodge.org/store.html
or email turtlelodge@ mts.net.

Most Trafford titles are also available at major online book retailers.

Elders' Teachings

This book is the Intellectual Property of those noted below and jointly owned and held in common.
Use or sharing of this material in whole or in part requires the consent of, and collective attribution to
Harry Bone, Sherry Copenace, Dave Courchene, William Easter, Robert Greene and
Henry Skywater, with contributions from Peter Atkinson and D'Arcy Linklater,
and original artwork by Henry Guimond.

Printed in the United States of America.

ISBN: 978-1-4669-3798-7 *(s)*

978-1-4669-3797-0 *(e)*

Library of Congress Control Number: 2012908705

Trafford rev. 05/21/2012

 www.trafford.com

North America & international
toll-free: 1 888 232 4444 (USA & Canada)
phone: 250 383 6864 ♦ fax: 812 355 4082

Contents

1.INTRODUCTION

We, the Elders, have done our best to represent our Red Nation as Ojibway, Cree and Dakota. We take full responsibility for what we have shared and written in the following pages. We present this story knowing it is an attempt to capture the fullness, richness and beauty of the Red Nation.

We have attempted to share our understanding as the Red People. We acknowledge the fact that we could never transfer our way of life through written words alone. We are an oral people. Sacred law cannot be written. It must be spoken and heard. Our way of life is meant to be lived and experienced. Our words are meant to inspire and guide our fellow human beings to follow the path of the heart.

We believe that the Creator has always been within our reach and that we have to connect to the Earth to be guided to our true purpose.

We believe that the spirit of the original Red Man was lowered to Mother Earth and our spirit chose to be born on Turtle Island. In all our languages, the Red People are referred to as the People of the Heart and the Land.

We do not own the Earth. How can anyone own their Mother? We owe our existence to Mother Earth.

This story tells of our human life and journey until our return back to the spirit world.

We believe that the Creator has always been within our reach and that we have to return to the Earth to be guided to our true purpose.

There are many Creation stories. We are told that every Creation story is true. How do we know this? We know this because the Creator told us this. The Creator comes to us through our dreams and our visions, and through the actual voice of the Earth itself. The trees speak to us, the animals speak to us. For us as the Red People, we regard nature as the voice and face of the Creator.

This book has been written by those of us residing very close to the geographical centre of the continent of Turtle Island (North America). At the very centre lies a very ancient sacred site, *Manito Api*, which the Red People of this area refer to as "Where the Creator Sits." It is located in the Whiteshell Provincial Park at Bannock Point, Manitoba, Canada.

Since time immemorial our nations have gathered on our sacred sites. They gathered to share knowledge, ceremonies, prophecies and dreams, dreams that affected all peoples.

"Where the Creator Sits" is a very significant sacred site of pilgrimage where the people had gathered to stay connected to the spirit and the land. When we activate the sacred site through our prayers and connection, we activate our own spirit as we connect to the spirit of the Creator in the land.

Sacred Site of "Where the Creator Sits" (*Manito Api*) at Bannock Point,
Whiteshell Provincial Park, Manitoba, Canada

Our prophecies tell of a time when all four races of humanity will reunite in the centre, and led by the Red People, return to the sacred ways that were given to us by the Creator. All four races of humanity will bring forward the gifts that each was given by the Creator to bring a higher understanding of what it means to be human and our purpose on this Earth.

Where the Creator sits is in the heart of all humanity. The heart is the centre of our being and the Creator sits in each of us. In the centre of the continent, we connect with our own centre, our heart, to the Creator who sits in the centre of our spirit.

Situated very close to the sacred site of "Where the Creator Sits", in the city of Winnipeg in Manitoba, lies what is known as the Forks. The meeting place of two rivers – the Red River and the Assiniboine, the Forks has been a very significant meeting place for the Red People for thousands and thousands of years. The Red Nations used to use the river systems to travel and meet at the Forks before making their journey of pilgrimage to the sacred site of "Where the Creator Sits" at the centre of the continent, located nearby.

The Forks also represents that in present time we have reached a time of decision. Do we continue to walk only a material life, or do we choose to build a world that has a spiritual foundation, a foundation that the Red People are willing to share, that is inclusive to all people?

Through ceremony, the Elders have been given the symbol of the Grandmother Turtle to be the one that will bring the story of the journey of the Red People. Our Creation Story tells us that the back of the turtle – Turtle Island – arose out of the water that covered our planet after the spirit of the Grandmother Turtle agreed to be the place to host Mother Earth.

To our people, the turtle is a symbol of truth, and the markings on her back confirm that truth. On the back of the turtle we see thirteen sections, representing the thirteen cycles of the moon that it takes for the Earth to revolve around the sun. We also see twenty-eight markings circling the shell of the turtle, representing the cycle of a woman and the cycle of the moon. The turtle carries our knowledge as a people. Her shell represents the protection of that knowledge.

It is with the help of the turtle and in the spirit of truth that we share our journey and our perspective of life with the people. We have come through a period of great darkness and endured to bring forward our contribution to humanity.

This is our story.

2. THE GREAT BEGINNING

Before the Creator

There are many Creation stories. We are told that they are all true.

This teaching was told to Weynabooshoo, Original Man. When Weynabooshoo was doing his work of naming everything on Turtle Island he asked this question. It was the very first time the question was asked: "Where does life come from?" Who did Weynabooshoo ask? He asked the Creator. And so the Creator and Grandmother Moon sat down with him and they told him this teaching.

In the beginning there was a time before the Creator was the Creator. Weynabooshoo was told that in the beginning there was darkness, there was nothing and there was no sound.

Out of the darkness came a sound, and the sound was like the sound of a shaker, shaking the seeds of life. We know now that this was the sound of Creation. Everything in the universe came from that darkness and that sound.

The sound came forward and traveled through four levels. When it went through the first level it became thought. Then it went through the second level where it became awareness. Then it traveled through the third level where it became awareness of being. When it traveled through the fourth level it became the Spirit.

Everything that we see on Earth and in the universe – the planets, the water, rocks, trees, plants, animals – everything came from the darkness just like the sound did. The Spirit then put in place the nine planets, and he became the Creator.

The Creation Story

The Creator then asked the question, "How will our children look?" Who was he asking? He was asking himself. In our teachings we now know that there is a duality in everything, so the Creator is then male and female; a duality that is the foundation of a relationship. The female part of the Creator then said "I will go find out," so she left and went into the darkness. Sometimes it is said that the Creator sent out his thoughts into the darkness, but there was nothing out there in the darkness for his thoughts to bounce back from, so he called them back. His thoughts are the stars we see at night, returning to him.

The question "How will our children look" was still unanswered. At this time, from one of the planets, *Wasi a bik* came forward and said that he would help. *Wasi abik* is the crystal rock. So *Wasi a bik* stood in front of the Creator, and the Creator looked into *Wasi a bik*, and for the first time ever there was a reflection. What the Creator saw was a beautiful blue light. We all have that blue light inside us, because we are all a part of the Creator. So now, they knew how their children would look. The Creator, that blue light, is at the centre of everything.

We are all made of this blue light. The real essence of us as humans is this blue light, which is our spirit. When the Creator had the original vision of life, he created us in the image of himself. The Creator gave each of us the gift and power to have vision and to make our visions real. We are in essence mini-Creators. The central purpose of our human life is to reflect who the Creator is, which is to bring respect and love into this world.

The Creator now knew how his children would look. There would be four different colours of man – Red, Yellow, Black and White. The Creator made a place for them that was Mother Earth. He told his children, "I have prepared a beautiful place for you to go to."

The White Man chose to be placed in Europe. The Black Man chose Africa. The Yellow race chose Asia. The Red Man chose to be placed in this part of the world, on what we call Turtle Island.

All were lowered to Earth to their homelands.

The spirit of the Red Man did not want to leave the Creator. The Creator said, "I have made a place for you to go to." So the spirit of the Red Man turned and slowly walked away.

He reached the first level from the Creator. At that level he stopped and turned around and told the Creator that he did not want to leave. The Creator said, "Go, go, my son. "

"I have prepared a beautiful place for you," said the Creator. So the spirit again turned and walked away.

He reached the second level, and again he turned and looked at the Creator and said he did not want to leave. The Creator then said, "Go, go, my grandson." The spirit turned again and walked away.

He reached the third level. Again he turned and told the Creator that he did not want to leave his side. Again the Creator said, "Go, go, my nephew."

The spirit then turned again and walked away very slowly and came to the fourth level from the Creator. Here he turned again and told the Creator that he did not want to leave him. The Creator said, "Go, go, my relative."

Then the Creator said, "I have made a place for you to go to, but because you do not want to leave me, I will put someone there that will teach you how to return to me, to return home where you came

from. He is the first spirit that greets you on your journey to Mother Earth and where your teachings begin." So the Creator put the Spirit of the Heart at the fourth level to sit and watch over us.

At the second level where the Red Man had stopped and looked back, the Creator placed an Everlasting Lake, and a female spirit to take care of the lake. At that level the spirit learns about the sacredness of water and that water is life. Water is the passage to life.

At the third level where the Red Man had stopped and turned around, the Creator placed Divine Spiritual Beings that would give the seven teachings on how to have a good life. These Divine Beings oversee life as it is being created and are there to greet the spirit as it arrives on Mother Earth, bringing the teachings.

At the fourth level the Creator placed the sun, the moon, the sky and the stars. Here the spirit sees the sun, the moon, the sky and the stars in relation to the significance that they will have in its human life.

The spirit of each human being has to go through all these four levels before entering the mother's womb. Already once the child has entered the mother's womb, its blue spirit comes in knowing how sacred life is, knowing all of these teachings contained in these four levels.

We are all spirits. We have already seen what we are going to do before we come to the Earth. We have already seen our challenges and our happinesses. We already know our purpose, our vision, our gifts and our destiny.

When we are born we deliberately forget what we have seen and what we have learned. Our blue spirit enters our human life learning what it means to be human. We already have all the knowledge and teachings inside us that will help us on our journey. It is our challenge as human beings to remember who we are as spirit, and to keep our blue spirit clear of all the negativities that surround us in life.

As we were being created, the Creator also gave each human spirit four gifts – its spiritual name, its clan, its way of life, and free will. In our teachings we talk of a loving Creator, not a punishing or a vengeful god, rather a beautiful spirit. The Creator provided teaching about how to live a good way of life, but loved us so much that he did not tell us we have to live that way. We can make our own choice as to how we will live this life.

The spirit was now ready to begin its journey on Mother Earth. The Creator lowered the spirit of man onto Mother Earth. She is female. This shows that woman preceded man.

The Red Man was born from Mother Earth. The spirit of the Red Man was lowered into a special plant from the water for the bear to eat. Over time and evolution, the bear gave birth to the Red Man, and that special plant was no longer needed for this reason.

3. JOURNEY OF THE HUMAN SPIRIT

We, the Elders, are sharing these teachings to bring forward the Red People's perspective on the journey and great potential of the human spirit. The way of life of the Red People was not destroyed – our people have persevered despite attempts to eradicate a way of life and the spirit of our people – to bring forward our contribution today.

There is a house in the heavens where I was born. It's me, it's me. The lightning beings are me. There is a house in the heavens. It's me, it's me.

Ancient Dakota song

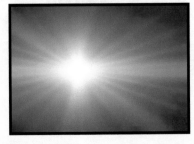

Dakota symbol for Heavens and Earth

There is a light from the heavens that enters the mother's womb (travelling from top right corner of triangle). The mother nurtures that spirit. The base of the triangle on the underside represents our walk in life. When our spirit finally returns to the spirit world, it forms the angle back up to the centre, to the house in the heavens (centre point of the triangle), before it finally makes the journey back to the Creator (the upper triangle).

The Four Elements of Nature

Every seed needs the four elements of Earth, air, water and fire to flourish into a flower, or a tree. Likewise, humanity and all of Creation depend upon the four elements of Nature for our spiritual, emotional, physical and mental survival and connection.

Earth

The Red People of Turtle Island have always been an Earth-based people. The close feelings and connection to the land has been a basis for our perspective on the meaning of and understanding of our relationship to life. "The Land is our Mother" is a simple but profound insight. It is the Earth who teaches and symbolizes the sacredness of the womb, the woman, the life-giver. It is the land that offers understanding of our beginning, our Creation, our oneness with Nature and each other as the human family. One human lifetime does not compare to the lifetime of Nature. The Earth does not belong to anyone – we all belong to the Earth. Nature operates on simple laws, that when followed, ensure a happy and balanced life.

Air

One's breath of life is a gift from the Great Spirit. The breath of life always means living in the present. How you live your life to the fullest is always determined by how you use that breath of life. It is not through recalling the past, nor through talk of future that life is meant to be enjoyed, but rather in the now, in the present. One must see and feel the blessings of the breath of the life as it passes through your whole being. As long as the breath of air passes through us, we are alive – alive to enjoy – alive to give – alive to care – alive to love.

Air is the sound. Air is the drum. The rattle is the air. The sound of the air creates vibration and connects us to the universe.

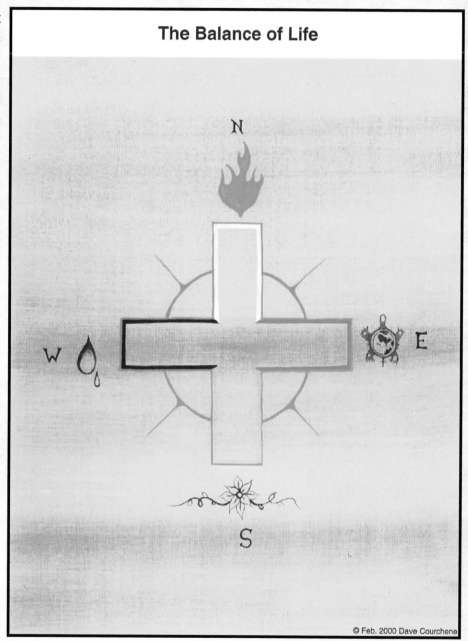

The Balance of Life

N

W

E

S

© Feb. 2000 Dave Courchene

Water

Water is the blood of Mother Earth. Water is life. Water offers the passage to life; it is the passage into the physical world during the time of birth of a child. Water is recognized as an element for purification, cleansing and helping to make peace. The spirits of the Thunderbirds bring the sacred water – the rains – to help cleanse and purify Mother Earth. For the Red People, it is the woman who has been given the responsibility of looking after and seeking the blessing of water.

Fire

The element of the sacred fire is central in the life of the Red People. Since the beginning, within the teachings of the Red People has been the sacred understanding of the power of fire.

The biggest fire of all is the sun, which reflects to us the symbol of our Great Creator. It is the Grandfather Sun that watches us throughout the day and then shines its light on Grandmother

Moon. It is the sun that brings the greatest light. It is the sun that brings a new birth and new beginning of innocence as we awake each morning.

When we light the sacred fire we bring a part of the sun very near to us. When we look at the sun it is like a doorway that opens for us to see the Creator shine upon all of us. The sacred fire has the power to open a doorway to the spiritual world. It is fire that ignites the flame in our hearts to closely connect to spirit. Without the sacred fire, there is darkness and doubt, and a person becomes cold, uncaring and selfish. It is the power of the fire that makes a person gentle and warm. When a person has been near a sacred fire many times, you will feel their warmth and compassion. You will feel the power of their words and actions simply because the light of the fire has been transferred to that individual.

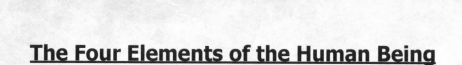

The Four Elements of the Human Being

The spirit enters into the womb to begin its journey as a human being, complete with emotions, body and mind. It takes nine moons for the human being to be created. When it enters into the human world, then these four elements must be nurtured equally, which ensures balance in life. When death arrives, the emotions, body and mind will be gone, but the spirit will move on, back where it has come from. It returns into the spirit world, which represents the complete circle of life.

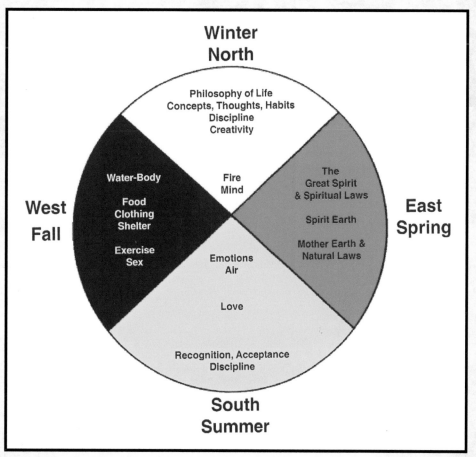

According to the teaching lodges of our people, we were told the Red People were given the special gift of understanding the spirit and our sacred relationship to the Earth. The Yellow People were given the gift of understanding emotions and air, the Black People were given understanding of the body and water, and the White People were given the gift of the mind and fire. Each race of people was given their special gifts to learn and understand in their deepest sense.

According to our prophecies as a people, a day will come in our evolution as humanity, when we will come together to share this knowledge. We will reach greater understanding as we represent our uniqueness as the four races of humankind.

The Four Stages of Life

In its human life, the spirit has the opportunity to live through the four stages of life – the Child, the Youth, the Adult and the Elder – before it returns to the spirit world. When the Child arrives, the Child is to be positioned at the centre of the family, the community and the nation. Every Child is born with the right to be human.

The right to be human is the right for a Child to be given all that it needs to be supported in its spirit, its emotions, its body and in its mind, so that when it is finally ready to be on its own it will have had all the nurturing and teachings it needs to survive.

In the natural world the mother bear will do everything to protect its cub, and she will teach her cub everything that will help the cub to survive later on when it must leave its mother's side. Only the mother will decide when the cub is ready, she will know when her cub has been provided what it needs to go out into the world on its own.

It is the same for us as humans. Every Child is born with the right to be respected and loved. Every Child is born with the right to have a good mother and good father that know the sacred teachings and laws of the people. Every Child is born with the right to drink clean water and to have nature's natural foods. Every Child is born with the right to be told the truth. Every Child must also be supported and encouraged to live its free will. The teachings that are provided should encourage that Child to be responsible for its own life once it goes out on its own.

The role of the Young people is to seek vision that will define their purpose and meaning and life, and to develop the gifts that identify their uniqueness and purpose.

The Adults are the ones that bring life into this world. Their responsibility is to live their role as parents, extended to aunties and uncles, supporting the life of the Child that is at the centre.

The Elders of the nation have always acted as mentors. They were always the inspirers, mentors and teachers of sacred law. The Elders are there to give guidance and direction to the young people, to ensure that sacred law is lived by. The Youth and the Elders should and must work together to ensure a solid foundation for the future.

The Four Seasons

The Red People have always followed the influence of the four seasons. The four seasons always reflected an understanding of balance.

Springtime is renewal and our new year – it is an exciting time to see Nature return to its beginning. It is a time to see the birds return to their birth place to give birth to their young. Our whole nature as human beings can feel this as we get closer to the land. It is a time to plant. Planting a seed on the land requires a faith and belief that the land will nurture this seed into an abundance of food.

Summertime offers a time to be really close to the land. The more time spent outside, the more enjoyment we experience in life. This is a time of great activity when we are literally working for life.

Fall time is a time for harvesting. It is a time for preparing for the winter months, preserving the foods, and hunting for the meat, picking and preparing the wild rice. It is a time to show gratitude for the abundance received from the land. It is a time when Feasts are done. It is a time to remember the ancestors. It is a time for nature to celebrate its own life through colour!

Wintertime is a time of resting and learning. Everything slows down, as does Nature, but life is still filled with activity done at a more natural pace yet filled with excitement. It is a time to spend a lot of time with the teachers – the grandmothers and grandfathers. It is a time of storytelling. There is always work – work keeps human beings healthy and strong. One can feel the winds of the north and the strength they offer. Wintertime also brings us the longest night that greets the new sun, as we begin again in the circle of life.

The Duties and Responsibilities of the Women and the Men

© Feb. 2000 Dave Courchene

The Women are the first contact for the Children. They are the creators of life. They groom the Children to be the leaders that carry the Seven Teachings. The Women give the language to the Child. The Women are the connection to Mother Earth.

The Men have been given the duty and responsibility to protect life, which includes all life – the Earth, the plant life, the animal life, and the human life.

4. SACRED LAWS

Original instruction was given to everything, not just people. The Creator put its spirit into us, so when he created the first human being, he put all his thoughts into that being including his Laws – his original instructions – that govern all of the universe. He also gave us Laws of the Land that we would learn from Mother Earth. He gave us Laws of the People, which would be based on these Laws of the Land, that would help us stay in balance and connected to him.

The head of the turtle represents the Creator, the source of our spirit of life. The body of the turtle represents Mother Earth. The tail represents us, the people; using our free will and the laws we were given as people to direct our life on Earth. The four legs represent the four directions, and the movement of the turtle, which requires four gifts we were given as a people – our language, our history, our way of life, our teachings and our ceremonies.

Laws of Creator

The Great Binding Law

The Great Binding Law is the Law of the Creator that binds all of Creation – the whole universe, the stars, Mother Earth, all of life. It covers everybody and everything. Although the law is comprised of many aspects, each of its parts operates independently and also interdependently. It applies to all things. It goes right down to the DNA of everything. The Great Binding Law is really the unconditional love that connects everything.

The spirit world is right in front of us. It is so close that we can reach into it. When the spirit returns it is a transformation from one life to another. The spirit world is right here with us. Wherever there is life, the Creator is there.

For everything he created, the Creator gave an instruction, an original instruction, about how we were to go about living. To the pine tree, the Creator gave an instruction about how to be a pine – the shape of its needles, how it was to bear branches, everything the pine needed to be a pine. It was the same for all the things in Creation – each was given original instruction.

So it was with the human beings. For each people, the Creator placed all things necessary to support and nourish our lives. For each people, the Creator gave an instruction, an original instruction, about how we were to go about on Mother Earth as human beings. Each people were given its languages, its teachings, its way of life, and its ceremonies.

The original instructions were the same for us all – these were to bring peace and love into the world, to respect Mother Earth, to put all children at the centre of our lives, and to walk the path of the heart.

Just as the pine tree never tries to convince the oak tree to change its ways, so it is that the original people never tell each other what they should do and believe. We welcome each other, each following our special ways.

The Seven Teachings

1. **1st Teaching: RESPECT represented by the BUFFALO**

Buffalo ● RESPECT

The Buffalo stands on guard to remind us of the teaching of Respect. Respect all life on Mother Earth, respect Elders and people of all races. The essence of respect is to give and share.

The buffalo embodies respect by giving of itself. The buffalo, through giving its life and sharing every part of its being, showed the deep respect it had for the people.

No animal was more important to the existence of Red families than the buffalo. A single buffalo could provide food, shelter, clothing and utensils for daily living. The Red People were true conservationists for they lived in a sustainable relationship with the buffalo and they believed themselves to be true caretakers of the great herds. This sustainable and mutual relationship with the buffalo resulted in a relationship that was a true expression of respect.

This spirit of respect was shown toward all of life because the Red People saw the interconnectedness of all life. They saw very clearly their dependence on the land. Therefore, the land and its resources were to be given absolute respect.

The essence of respect means having the ability to give. To show respect to life, you simply give of yourself. You can serve your fellow human beings by giving of yourself for the betterment of humanity and for the betterment of the world.

The biggest secret of life is to give and to share. What we give returns to us multifold in many ways. What is important is not what we have, what is important is what we give. When we show respect we become free from materialism. It is considered the highest honour is to serve others, to serve humanity, to serve life.

2. 2nd Teaching: LOVE represented by the EAGLE

Eagle ● LOVE

The Eagle welcomes all with the spirit of Love. The wings spread in welcome. Love is the essence of life. Always act in love. Love the Creator. Love Mother Earth. Love yourself, your family, and your fellow human beings.

To feel true love is to know the Creator. It is understood that one's first love must be the Creator. He is considered the father of all children, the giver of the life enjoyed by a human being. Love expressed and given to the Creator is shown by loving yourself and how the Creator made you. It is only when you love yourself that you can truly love someone else. Children are to be loved and cherished, for children are the gifts from the Creator.

The eagle to the Red People represents the spirit of love. Just as the eagle flies the highest, love represents the highest form of our humanity. The eagle is a bird that flies the highest to reflect the relationship that it has with the highest power of Spirit. It has always been the most revered bird for the Red People. The old people would say, "Rise as high as the eagle and you will have vision and see more." Symbolically the eagle is the one who can reach the highest in bringing vision and love to the seeker. Pure vision from the Creator is the most treasured and sought after. Love is considered the greatest and most powerful healing agent. The feeling of love becomes our constant need in life. We want to feel love, we want to give love.

For the Red People, the eagle and his feathers help bring that spirit of love and vision. In Red society, the true leaders of the people carry a staff filled with eagle feathers. The leader is expected to lead his people in love. The leader spends years training spiritually, knowing the Seven Teachings, learning, participating in and leading many ceremonies. He spends time on the land, many times alone, to ensure his close connection to the land – to the mother, Mother Earth.

3. **3rd Teaching: COURAGE represented by the BEAR**

Bear ● COURAGE

The Bear stands tall to remind us of the teaching of Courage. Listen to your heart. It takes courage to do what is right.

To have courage is to have the mental and moral strength to listen to the heart. To have courage is to overcome fears that could prevent us from living our true spirit as human beings. In the natural world, the bear shows us the spirit of courage. By nature this animal is very gentle, but if you show any sign of approaching a bear cub a mother bear will display total fearlessness in defending her child.

The bear represents living from the heart – living your spirit. The bear is very close to the land and has brought many medicines to the people. The bear is an example of courage – the courage needed to seek vision.

It was the bear that taught the Red People the importance of fasting. The Red People learned about the Vision Quest ceremony from watching the bear fast. In the fall, the bear goes into the land to hibernate. Red people do not understand it this way – to our people the bear has gone to fast. The bear in its yearly ritual returns to the land to fast to ensure the Creator's vision is kept alive – that life continues on Mother Earth. The bear allows Mother Earth her rest time by not taking from her in the winter months. From the bear we learn that the more one is able to fast, the more balanced one becomes. It is also much easier to connect with spirit when you cleanse your body of unnatural elements by fasting. Many Indigenous ceremonies involve fasting. It is in ceremony that people can seek the spiritual strength to be courageous enough to live their vision and to have the courage to love themselves.

It sometimes takes a lot of courage to listen to your heart and to your spirit as it is telling you what to do even when your mind tells you something else. We all need courage to do the right thing. When there is courage there can be the power to change what is destroying life. The bear represents the courage that is needed to show love and respect to the land and life.

4. **4th Teaching: HONESTY represented by the SABÉ (BIGFOOT)**

Sabé (Bigfoot) ●HONESTY

The Sabé holds its heart to remind us to live in honesty – to live from the heart. Never lie or gossip. Be honest with yourself and others. Speak from your heart. Be true to your word.

The essence of honesty is innocence. Honesty means being an honourable person free from fraud or deceptions. Honesty means a refusal to lie, steal or deceive in any way. The highest honour that can be bestowed upon an individual in Red society is the saying, "There walks an honest man: he can be trusted." Elders will say, "Never try to be someone else—live true to your spirit – be honest with yourself, accept who you are and the way Creator made you."

The Sabé, which represents this teaching, symbolically reflects the understanding of honesty. The more honest you are the bigger you become as a person. Long ago, there was a giant called Kitchi Sabé who walked among the people to remind them to be honest to the teachings of the Creator and to each other. To be truly honest was to keep one's promise made to the Creator and to be as good as one's word. To be considered "a man of his word" was honourable.

The Creator chose the Sabé to represent the teaching of honesty. Perhaps the reason why the spirit of Sabé is so elusive is because it is very hard to be honest. We see it and then it is gone, as the Sabé moves from the spiritual to the physical form, in the same way that honesty is elusive. It is only in acknowledging and becoming one with the land that we have an opportunity to feel our spirit and live in honesty.

The Elders say the best way you can show honesty or honour the spirit of the Sabé, is to speak from your heart and listen to your spirit that has given you the inspiration of the words you are to speak. When you are honest with yourself, you are true to the words that you speak.

5. WISDOM represented by the BEAVER

Beaver ●WISDOM

The Beaver brings the teaching of Wisdom. Everyone has been given a special gift. Show wisdom by using your gift to build a peaceful world.

To know and understand wisdom is to know the Creator gave everyone special gifts which were to be used to serve life, to serve humanity and to build a peaceful and healthy community. The beaver represents that building. The beaver uses his special gift received from the Creator (his sharp teeth) for cutting trees and branches, which he uses for building dams and lodges and changing the landscape. If the beaver did not use his gift to build, and lay on the shore while the other beavers were working, his teeth would grow so long that they would become useless, he would be unable to eat, and he would physically die.

It is the same for us as human beings. If you do not use your gifts, your spirit would become weak because you are not fulfilling their use. This denial eventually leads to sickness because each human being's special gifts help impart self-worth and identity. You would become sick, mentally, emotionally or physically.

Beaver reflects the wisdom of using one's own Creator-given gifts properly to build a peaceful, healthy world community.

6. **6th Teaching: HUMILITY Represented by the WOLF**

Wolf ● HUMILITY

The Wolf bows its head in humbleness as it brings us the teaching of Humility, to show us all that we have been created equal in the eyes of the Creator. No one is greater or lesser in the human family. Think of others before yourself. Humble yourself to the Creator by being thankful.

To be truly humble is to recognize, acknowledge and honour a Higher Power than man – one whom we call the Creator, the Great Spirit, the highest source of power that exists. Humility is reflecting and expressing a spirit of deference or submission to the Creator. To be humble is to understand we are equal in the eyes of the Creator through His unconditional Love for all of us. The Creator's Love is expressed to all of us in the same way that the sun will shine on us all. The sun does not choose to shine on any one person alone or any one race of people; it shines on all.

There are many paths to the Creator. One path is not greater or lesser than another. We humble ourselves by accepting these paths leading to the same Creator for all of us.

The wolf echoes humbleness in the natural world, by knowing, acknowledging and practising that in the eyes of the Creator we are all equal under his great love for all living beings. When encountering another animal or human being, the wolf bows his head not because he is afraid, but because he is humble – the wolf is showing humbleness in the presence of the other animal or human being. A wolf that has hunted for food will take his food back to the den to eat with the pack before he takes the first bite of food.

The teaching of humility is very important in life. Much of the division we see in today's world is because people have not understood the teaching of humility. Practicing humbleness means to always consider our fellow human beings before ourselves. Humility is a teaching to prevent against an attitude of arrogance and superiority. To understand humility is to understand that no one is greater or lesser than another human being in this life.

7. TRUTH Represented by the Turtle

Turtle ●TRUTH

The Turtle brings the teaching of Truth. Always seek Truth. Living the Truth is living all these teachings – Respect, Love, Courage, Honesty, Wisdom and Humility. Let us join together to help fulfill the prophecy of the Red people – coming together as a human family to bring truth into the world.

The seventh and final teaching that we were given is represented by the turtle. The teaching that the Grandmother Turtle carries is the teaching of truth.

To know truth is to know and understand all the original seven spiritual teachings as given by the Creator, and to remain faithful to these teachings. The Creator really is the "Truth, the whole Truth and nothing but the Truth."

The essence of truth is freedom – found in each of us living our true spirits, living from the heart. According to our understanding, the meaning and the essence of truth are all the Seven Teachings put together: Truth is respect, truth is love, truth is courage, truth is honesty, truth is wisdom, and truth is humility. The converse is also true: you cannot have truth without respect; you cannot have truth without love; you cannot have truth without courage; you cannot have truth without honesty; you cannot have truth without wisdom; and you cannot have truth without humility.

The First Peoples believe that the Creator chose the turtle to hold remembrance of all the teachings, the teachings, and our natural relationship to Mother Earth and the Spirit. It is said that in the beginning, when the Creator made human beings he gave us Seven Teachings to live by they would guide us to the truth and meaning of our life on Earth. As he gave us these teachings, the Grandmother Turtle was present when the teachings were presented to the Red People, to ensure that they would never be lost or forgotten. The turtle is one of the oldest animals. It has lived past the many changes the Earth has undergone. This is a testament in itself – truth will always prevail. The Grandmother Turtle teaches the enduring power of truth.

The shell of the turtle represents the body of real events, teachings and origins of the human being. On the back of the turtle are thirteen sections which represent the truth of one cycle of thirteen moons in the Earth's yearly rotation around the sun. Thirteen also represents the four seasons in the Earth's cycle around the sun, plus the nine months it takes for the gestation of a human child in the mother's womb.

There are also twenty-eight markings on the back of the turtle which represent the cycle of one moon, and the length of time of the menstrual cycle of a woman. These signs are a confirmation of the truth which the turtle reflects.

The turtle is a symbol of all our Red Nations. Our people have referred to North America as Turtle Island, a reference to the truth. The Turtle Lodge in Sagkeeng First Nation, Manitoba, Canada, near the centre of Turtle Island, was built in the shape of a turtle based on a vision received. Like the turtle, who is one of the oldest animals, having survived even the dinosaur age, the power of truth has survived the test of time. It is only today, for the first time in the history of our planet, that the turtle is being threatened by pollution of water and Mother Earth's environment. It is believed by our people that it is here on Turtle Island that the truth of man's existence and meaning of life will be revealed.

For the Red People, the turtle is like a grandmother. The grandmother is the power of the nation. She represents the spirit of the people, the woman, and the land. Like no one else, she is able to love, to nurture and to discipline the children of the nation. The Red People refer to the grandmothers as "beings of kindness", who in their grandmotherhood have become closest to understanding the Spirit, the land, and the teachings that comprise truth.

Laws of the Land

As the Red People, we are defined by our relationship with Mother Earth. The relationship is not worship, but rather an understanding and acknowledgement of how the Earth sustains life in all forms. We believe Mother Earth is a living entity with a spirit. The Red People were given the gift of understanding the significance of spirit and our sacred relationship with the Earth. The spirit within each of us connects us to Mother Earth. Because all of Creation has a spirit, a spark of the divine, we are always in the presence of the Creator.

We are an extension of the Earth. Many people today have disconnected themselves from the Earth to become a separate entity. It is by connecting to Mother Earth that we connect to the divine and to our original purpose as human beings.

We do not own the Earth. We owe our existence to the Earth. She does not need us yet we need her to survive. The health of the planet is directly connected to the well-being of humanity. The land sustains us and nourishes us. Being connected to the Earth and having a relationship with the Earth helps people to stay balanced. The way of life of the Red People gives us a close connection to the Earth that enables us to understand and hear the voice of Mother Earth.

Everyone whether they acknowledge it or not has a relationship with Mother Earth. The land has a way of bringing harmony. We believe that all of humanity is drawn to the Earth. The propensity for cottage living is an example of the pull toward the Earth; seeking solace by being close to nature. Only the plants and the animals are following the natural order of living within the cycles of the Earth. Even they, however, are feeling the effects of humanity's disruption of nature. If everybody understood that each of us has a personal relationship with the land and treated the land as though their life depended on it, which it surely does, the exploitation of the Earth would stop and a new economic order would emerge out of a way of life that is anchored in sacred spiritual law.

Humanity needs to acknowledge the Earth as a living entity with the same attributes as ourselves. We need to come to terms as a human race that our relationship with Mother Earth is the same as our relationship with our mothers and all other living beings.

Nature operates on the principle of balance. Since time immemorial, the Red people survived by following **Laws of the Land**, also known as Natural Laws, which helped us to live in balance and harmony.

Reflected in the circle and cycles of life, Laws of the Land are learned by observing Mother Earth. The circle is a part of nature and also a reflection of our identity. Everything happens in cycles. Nature reminds us of the power of the circle, such as in the tornado. We recognize the power of the circle because it strengthens and protects us. Nature keeps repeating herself so that we come to understand balance. We are supposed to follow Laws of the Land so we stay balanced and connected to the land.

The sun rising every morning is a Law of the Land.

The cycle of the seasons is a Law of the Land.

The cycle of the moon is a Law of the Land.

Gravity is a Law of the Land.

The flow of the water and the cycle of the tides are Laws of the Land.

The woman that bleeds every month in order to maintain her gift to create life is a Law of the Land.

There are two parts to everything we see on Earth, female and male, a duality. In that duality is the foundation of a relationship – a foundation of respect. This is a Law of the Land.

The cycle of the Earth requires the cycle of thirteen moons to revolve around the sun. This is a Law of the Land. Nine of these moons represent the gestation period of a child in the womb of its mother. The remaining four moons represent the balance of life: the four quadrants – the four seasons, the four elements of Nature, the four elements of the human being, the four stages of life, and the four races.

Until humanity learns how to honour Laws of the Land we will not know how to walk on the Earth. We need to find a way to synchronize our life with the cycles of nature and the four elements of Earth, air, water and fire.

As children of the Earth we rely on our Mother the Earth to teach us, correct us, guide us and give us sustenance for our physical life. The Earth manifests the spirit of the Great Spirit. By learning Laws of Land, we learn that:

We have evolved and continue to evolve from the land.

We are the land.

The land is our primary teacher for understanding our roles as human beings.

The land gives us what we need to live and survive.

We must only take what we need to live. If we take more than we need we must share it immediately.

As long as a child is born it means Nature can provide for its life.

The land provides true healing.

The land teaches humbleness.

The land teaches the importance of balance in life.

We are all children of the Earth. We all come from the land. If we human beings misbehave and do not follow Laws of the Land, Mother Earth will be the one to correct and bring us back to sacredness. For example, with the construction of dams we have tampered with the Law of the Land that water naturally follows. When we attack the land, we are told that whatever we do to our mother will manifest in us. To look after the Earth is to care for ourselves.

Laws of the People

The Red People have been given many gifts by the Creator. Our life is a gift. Everything representing the support of life is a gift.

We have been told through our sacred lodges and ceremonies that each people were given four original gifts – our language, our way of life, our teachings and our ceremonies. These gifts help us on our human journey of our spirit on Earth. Our Laws as a People are derived from our connection to the land and the Creator.

Language

Language given to us by the Creator brings sacred law and sacred teachings. Through our language is derived sacred understanding. We are an oral people, and our languages convey the spirit of our teachings, heart to heart.

Everything we talk about in our original languages is a reflection of life. The word for water in many of our languages is connected to the meaning of life. Water means "I am life". Indeed, out of the water comes life. We are all born from the water.

Our languages are rooted in the land and are derived from the land itself. Mother Earth speaks to us with the language of life. She gives us the teachings we need to live in balance. Those of us who listen can hear her voice. The trees speak to us, the wind speaks to us, the rocks speak to us, the plants and the animals speak to us. Everything we know we learn from the land and what is on the land. We read from the land, the land teaches us, that is where the voices come from.

We say there are four levels of language. The first level is the language we speak to each other in our daily conversations.

The second level is the language we speak to the Spirit, in prayer, for example, in a pipe ceremony. This is a deeper, more profound way of speaking. Our languages are directly connected to our ceremonies. The language of ceremonies is different from everyday conversational language.

The third level is the language used to interpret the language the Spirit speaks to us, such as in our most sacred ceremonies. The teachings provided through our ceremonies are in a spiritual language. They can be interpreted only by those who can understand the language. Sometimes the words that are used in ceremony are not used in the everyday language, and need to be interpreted even if you speak the language.

The fourth level of language is the language of dreams. For us as a people, dreams and visions have always provided guidance and direction directly from the spirit world, from the Creator. This language speaks directly to our spirit. It is different than the other levels of language.

The source of who we are as a people can be understood through our languages. When we speak, sing and pray in our original languages we connect to the spirit of the land that is the spirit of the Creator.

Way of Life

In Mother Earth, the Creator gave us everything we need to look after ourselves. We were given our way of life that we learned about as our blue spirit made its journey through those four levels on its way here. We were given our sacred laws and understanding, our gifts and our teachings. Our way of life is also about our duties and responsibilities to ourselves, our children, our families, our communities and to our nations. Our way of life is all about how we make this journey through our life on Earth – how we transfer those spiritual understandings that are inside us to our physical life as human beings, complete with spirit, emotions, body and mind, and connected to our Mother the Earth.

Teachings

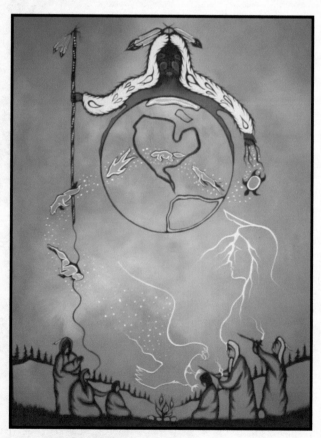

Our teachings are the specific things that we learn about specific ways how to live our lives and how to do our ceremonies. We have teachings for everything about how to live our lives as individual people, right from conception until we leave this Earth. We have teachings for pregnancy, teachings for childhood, youth, adulthood and elderhood, and teachings for men and for women. Teachings are unique to each people on Earth, but are still derived from one Creator.

Our teachings tell us we have duties and responsibilities that we carry out within the framework of the Seven Teachings: to ourselves, to others, to the land, nature and animals upon which we depend for our survival.

Our teachings come from the Creator and Mother Earth. Our spirit already has knowledge of our teachings, which were transferred to us from those four levels we came through on our journey here. We learn our teachings through the Divine Beings that continue to come to us through the voice of Mother Earth, in our ceremonies, and in our dreams and visions. The elders and wisdom keepers of our nations are keepers of our teachings, and help mentor us and give us guidance and direction.

Ceremonies

Our ceremonies are our ways of honouring and acknowledging our connection to the Creator and Mother Earth, our language, our way of life, and our teachings. Through ceremony we honour and show gratitude for those four levels that our blue spirits came through on our journey here. We stay connected to our Sacred Laws through ceremony. Our relationship with the land always includes prayer and ceremony in recognition that everything has a spirit and is therefore sacred. Ceremony helps us to stay balanced and connected with the forces of the universe. Ceremony tells us how to live with other people and to honour the land, for example, by offering tobacco when we take plants and doing ceremony when we take

animals.

Life itself should be a ceremony, an ongoing acknowledgement and remembrance of the Creator all the time. It is a way of living, thinking and being.

When we enter into ceremony we enter into prayer. We have a power called belief. Prayer connects us to the Creator, with the spirit. If we can connect with the spirit we can heal ourselves, fulfill our dreams, and change the world.

Makoose Ka Win Young Women's Rites of Passage Painting courtesy Henry Guimond, © Turtle Lodge 2010

Ceremony is so important. Ceremony strengthens belief and faith. Ceremony is essential in one's life, simply because it offers a strong reminder of one's spiritual connection. The more one is able to find one's self in ceremony, the stronger one's spirit becomes.

The spiritual ceremonies given to the Red People are Earth-based, reflecting the connection to the natural world and its Laws of the Land.

Ceremony ensures a close connection to the Divine Beings. It is through repeated ceremony that we invoke and maintain a close connection with these Divine Beings for continued guidance and direction.

As a people we have many ceremonies. Pipe ceremonies, smudging ceremonies, rites of passage, water ceremonies, sacred fire ceremonies, the sweat lodge and the Sundance ceremonies and ceremonies to honour our ancestors are examples of some of our special ceremonies.

5. GIFTS OF THE RED PEOPLE

Pipe

We are told in our sacred lodges by our elders and knowledge keepers that the holy White Buffalo Calf Woman appeared and brought the sacred pipe to the Red People at a time when they were having a hard time and their belief in the Creator was weakening, to encourage their spirituality. She gave instructions to use the gift of the pipe to communicate with and acknowledge the Creator, Mother Earth and the spirits of the four directions, and to call for their help and direction in times of need.

The pipe represents our relationship with the Creator, facilitates our communication and acknowledges, invokes and strengthens our relationship with the spirit. One points the pipe to acknowledge the spirit in seven directions – to the highest power of the Creator himself, to the spirit of Mother Earth, to the spiritual helpers and Divine Beings that live in the four directions, and, finally, to oneself as one acknowledges the spirit inside oneself.

The pipe also represents a clear reflection of the balance found in nature, represented by the woman and the man. The bowl of the pipe represents the woman and the stem represents the man. They have to be connected to have balance and to bring forward life.

Rattle

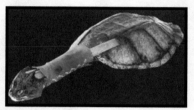

In our Creation Story, out of the darkness there came a sound. It was the sound of a shaker, shaking the seeds of life.

We believe the rattle is a gift that has been given to the Red People, to remind us and connect us to the sound of our Creation. Sounding the rattle invokes the Spirit to come and help us.

Drum

To the Red People, the drum represents the heartbeat. The drum is the sound of our own heartbeat, which reminds us of the first heartbeat we ever heard – that of our mother in her womb, and that of the mother of us all, Mother Earth.

The drum has the ability to awaken the human spirit and to speak to our hearts. Whenever we speak, the drum listens. Once it has heard, it then carries the message to all the people to be heard. The drum takes the message of peace that is delivered by the messengers into the hearts of the human beings. The drum opens the heart to receive the message spoken. It carries the voice and the prayers of the people. This is the power of the drum.

It is our belief that all people, not just the Red People, were given the gifts of the Pipe, Rattle and the Drum, but that is their story to discover and tell.

6. PROPHECIES

For us as the Red People, the Creator is the source of our visions and prophecies. Like all other peoples of the world, our people too have prophets. Our prophecies are not so much about predicting doom and gloom, rather they are visions of hope and inspiration that help guide the people to a greater understanding of life and our purpose as human beings in bringing love, respect, peace, beauty and harmony to the world.

The 8th Fire Prophecy

The Red People, the Ojibway, who live in this area at the centre of Turtle Island, carry a prophecy. The 8th fire prophecy shares that a time will come when Mother Earth will enter into a change and rebirth, a time of a "New Life". The Creator's love will speak through the forces of Nature, Mother Earth, to bring back balance and prevent the destruction of our planet. The Creator would never allow Mother Earth to be destroyed. At that time all cultures of the world will gather here at the centre of Turtle Island to share their teachings and knowledge and collectively seek a vision that would create a "New People" representing all races of humanity. The New People will find a way to unite and create a new understanding of how to live in peace and care for the Earth. At the heart of the understanding will be the Seven Teachings brought forward by the Red People, a lasting foundation upon which a peaceful world will be built.

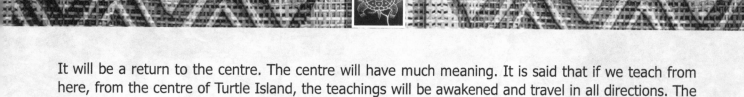

It will be a return to the centre. The centre will have much meaning. It is said that if we teach from here, from the centre of Turtle Island, the teachings will be awakened and travel in all directions. The centre acts as a metaphor that the Creator should be central in our lives.

The New Life will be heralded by a time of choice, when there will be an urgency for all of us to be reminded of our sacred responsibility to treat each other, all life and the Earth with more respect.

According to our Elders that are performing ceremonies, the Spirit has confirmed that the New Life has arrived.

Warriors of the Rainbow Prophecy[1]

The Cree people have a prophecy called the Warriors of the Rainbow prophecy. It is told that in the last century there lived a grandmother from the Cree tribe named "Eyes of Fire". She prophesied that one day, because of human greed, there will come a time, when the fish will die in the streams, the birds will fall from the air, the waters will be blackened, the trees will no longer be, and humankind as we will know it will all but cease to exist.

There will come a time when the keepers of the ceremonies, teachings, legends, stories, culture, rituals, and myths, and all the ancient tribal customs will be needed to restore us to health. They will be humankinds' key to survival, and they will be known as the "Warriors of the Rainbow".

They would not be warriors in the sense of using war or violence, rather enlightened human beings who would be dedicated to following a path of peace to bring love and respect back to Mother Earth.

---

1   Adapted from: Dr. Lelanie Fuller Anderson's website: http://www.angelfire.com/ok/TheCherokeeLady/warriorsrainbow.html

The prophecy shares that there will come a day of awakening when all the peoples of all the tribes will form a New World of justice, peace, freedom and recognition of the Great Spirit.

The Warriors of the Rainbow will spread these messages and teach all peoples of the Earth. They will teach them how to live the "Way of the Great Spirit". They will tell them of how the world today has turned away from the Great Spirit and that is why our Mother Earth is sick.

The Warriors of the Rainbow will show the peoples that this Great Spirit is full of love and understanding, and will teach them how to make the Earth beautiful again. These Warriors will give the people principles or rules to follow to make their path right with the world. These principles will be those of the ancient tribes. The Warriors of the Rainbow will teach the people of the ancient practices of unity, love and understanding. They will teach of harmony among people in all four corners of the Earth.

Like the ancient tribes, they will teach the peoples how to pray to the Great Spirit with love that flows like the beautiful mountain stream, and flows along the path to the ocean of life. Once again, they will be able to feel joy in solitude and in councils. They will be free of petty jealousies and love all humankind as their sisters and brothers, regardless of colour, race or religion. They will feel happiness enter their hearts, and become as one with the entire human race. Their hearts will be pure and radiate warmth, understanding and respect for all humankind, nature, and the Great Spirit. They will once again fill their minds, hearts, souls, and deeds with the purest of thoughts. They will seek the beauty of the Master of Life—the Great Spirit! They will find strength and beauty in prayer and the solitudes of life.

Their children will once again be able to run free and enjoy the treasures of nature and Mother Earth. Free from the fears of toxins and destruction, wrought by the human beings of the age past and his practices of greed. The rivers will again run clear, the forests will be abundant and beautiful, and the animals and birds will be replenished. The powers of the plants and animals will again be respected and conservation of all that is beautiful will become a way of life.

The poor, sick and needy will be cared for by their brothers and sisters of the Earth. These practices will again become a part of their daily lives. The leaders of the people will be chosen in the old way—not by their political party, or who is able to speak the loudest, boast the most, or by name calling or mud-slinging, but by those whose actions of love and kindness speak the loudest. Those who demonstrate their love, wisdom, and courage and those who show that they can and do work for the good of all, will be chosen as the leaders and chiefs. They will be chosen by their quality and not by the amount of money they have obtained. Like the thoughtful and devoted ancient leaders, they will understand the people with love, and see that their young are educated with the love and wisdom of their surroundings. They will show them that miracles can be accomplished to heal this world of its ills, and restore it to health and beauty.

The tasks of these Warriors of the Rainbow will be many and great. There will be terrifying mountains of ignorance to conquer and they shall find prejudice and hatred. They must be dedicated, unwavering in their strength, and strong of heart. They will find willing hearts and minds that will follow them on this road of returning Mother Earth to beauty and plenty once more.

It is said that this day will come, and that it is not far away. It will be the day that we shall see how we owe our very existence to Mother Earth and the people of all tribes, the Warriors of the Rainbow, that have maintained their culture and heritage. They are those that have kept the ceremonies, teachings, stories, legends, and myths alive. It will be with this knowledge, the knowledge that they have preserved, under the leadership of the Red Nations and yet with the equal participation of all Nations of humankind, that we shall once again return to harmony with nature, Mother Earth, and humankind. It will be with this knowledge that we shall find the key to our survival.

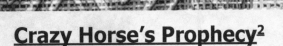

Crazy Horse's Prophecy[2]

The following is a prophecy carried by the Lakota Nation in the centre of Turtle Island, by one of their great leaders and prophets, Chief Crazy Horse. Chief Crazy Horse spoke these words as he smoked the Sacred Chanupa (Pipe) for the last time with Chief Sitting Bull, in 1877.

Upon suffering beyond suffering;

The Red Nation shall rise again.

It will be a blessing for a sick world

A world filled with broken promises, selfishness and separations

A world longing for light again!

I see a time, long after the skies have grown dark and dirty

And the Water has become bad-smelling

I see a time of seventh generation,

When all the colours of mankind

Will gather under the Sacred Tree of Life

And one whole Earth will become one Circle again.

In that day, there will be those among the Red Nation who will carry knowledge and understanding of unity among all living things, and the young White ones will come to those of my people and ask for this Wisdom.

I salute the light in your eyes

Where the whole universe dwells

For when you are at the centre within you and I am at that place within me, we shall be one.

— Chief Crazy Horse of the Lakota Nation

2   From: Indian Heroes and Great Chieftains by Charles Alexander Eastman, University of Nebraska Press, 1918.

Black Elk's Prophecy[3]

Black Elk (1863-1950), Holy Man of the Oglala (Lakota) also shared a vision he had which reflected a prophecy:

There I was standing on the highest mountain of them all, and round about beneath me was the whole hoop of the world.

And while I stood there I saw more that I can tell and I understood more than I saw;

For I was seeing in a sacred manner the shapes of all things that the sacred hoop of my people was one of many hoops that made one circle, wide as daylight and as starlight,

And in the centre grew one mighty flowering tree to shelter all the children of one mother and one father.

And I knew that it was holy.

3   From: Black Elk Speaks: Being the Life Story of a Holy Man of the Oglala Sioux by John G. Neihardt, University of Nebraska Press, 1988.

7. HUMANITY – 4 RACES COMING TOGETHER

The Elders of our Red Nations have confirmed that we have entered a time that the New Life of our 8th fire prophecy has arrived. They say that the New People are amongst us now. They are people represented by many cultures who have managed to find their purpose in helping to fulfill the dream of peace and love that the world is waiting for.

Each of us is being given the same opportunity today, now, to support the New Life by laying a foundation, founded on Sacred Law. For the first time in our human history, we are entering into a time where all races of humanity are joining together in unity, to become one and find truth as we represent the fullness of all of the gifts that we carry as different peoples.

It is here in the center of the continent of Turtle Island that the people of this area have referred to our sacred site of pilgrimage as "Where the Creator Sits". The Creator sits in the center of Turtle Island the same way as he sits in the center of our hearts. The reason the sacred site is here is to remind us that as we are at the centre, we must make that journey to our centre.

What you have heard is our story, our journey to the heart.

Our prophecies tell us that with the participation of the Red People and all peoples, the New People will somehow find a way to create a new understanding of how we should live and behave as human beings— where we will go beyond the division we have created amongst ourselves. We will find a way of life collectively to prevent the violence we see in our communities, on the street, and in our homes. There will be a spiritual understanding created that would go beyond the divisions and the separations that have caused the violence and wars today.

It is the role of the Elders and Adults to provide the right mentorship for the New People – the Youth of today – to gather to share the uniqueness of each of their strengths and bring forward the teachings and knowledge that they have gathered from their cultures that reflect balance in the circle of life. In supporting this New Life, we must learn to live from the heart. We must speak from the heart. We must act from the heart. Within the essence of our Spirit, all that we will need to support the New Life is within each of us.

Today we the Red People encourage everyone to put as much effort as we can into living from the true nature of our individual spirits, and connecting to the Creator through Mother Earth. We are challenged today to find a vision that is inclusive – a vision which supports all life that brings a spirit of hope for our future. As the Creator had the first vision, we have the same ability and power to have a vision that supports the original vision of life.

We offer these teachings, our perspective as the Red People, as an inspiration to return to our original purpose as humanity. The Red People brings a gift of opportunity to share the true spirit of love by honouring the uniqueness in the human family. We are all different but that difference does not mean we should be separated. What our people almost lost we the Elders are bringing forward today. The circle of life continues as we return to our original instructions, and we believe this time all the races of humankind will walk with us. Our prophecies have told us that it will be our people, the Red People, who will lead this movement of return.

We end as we began with the sound of the rattle – the sound of Creation – the sound of hope.

IMAGE INDEX

ABOUT THE AUTHORS

The following authors and contributors – Elders from the Ojibway (Anishnabe), Cree and Dakota Nations – met many times inside the **Turtle Lodge** to share and bring out the teachings and knowledge found in this book. The **Turtle Lodge** is a place of learning, healing and sharing ancient Indigenous knowledge for all peoples, focusing on the youth. It is located in Sagkeeng First Nation, Manitoba, Canada, and was built based on a vision received by Elder Dave Courchene (Nii Gaani Aki Inini – Leading Earth Man).

More information on the Turtle Lodge can be found at www.theturtlelodge.org and on our Facebook Page, "The Turtle Lodge".

Peter Atkinson - Dabasaaniqwat (Low Cloud) is from the Turtle Clan and has entered the Midewin lodge twice. Born in Roseau, Peter has a large family and does various ceremonies. He enjoys sharing teachings that were passed on to him.

Peter believes that the only way to effect change within our people is to follow the example of his ancestors, who left for us a positive way of thinking and many beautiful teachings. It is very important for him to share with our younger generation, as they will be the generation that will bring the teachings into the future.

Harry Bone (Giizis-inini from the Mikinaak Clan) is from Giizhigoowining (Keeseekoowenin) in Treaty No.2 territory. Fluent in Ojibway and English, he was the former Chief of Keeseekoowenin First Nation, CEO of West Region Tribal Council and Director of Education of Keeseekoowenin and the Manitoba Indian Education Authority.

Elder Bone has a special interest in the Treaties, specializes in First Nations Government, and has led delegations that have met with all levels of government. He has been instrumental in furthering the Treaty Education Initiative, Oral History Project and Historical Atlas of First Nations in Manitoba.

Sherry Copenace – Nii zho sake and Sa gi ma Kwe, Atik dodem (Elk clan) – was born and raised at Ojibways of Onigaming First Nation. She was raised by her parents, John and Evelyn Copenace, and lived next door to her paternal grandparents, Shawon and Mensinoiwshkung, who were very influential and provided many Anishinabe teachings to her.

Sherry is a firm believer and supporter of the Anishinabe way of life and speaks the Anishinabe language. She is the keeper of Paabamasagaa – the Treaty 3 Peoples Drum. She belongs to a large extended family and has two daughters, Gwen and Kara, and three grandchildren, Robyn, Valec John and Evey.

Dave Courchene - Nii Gaani Aki Inini (Leading Earth Man) has travelled internationally, carrying a message of hope and peace. Dave created a special place for sharing ancient Indigenous knowledge - the Turtle Lodge - based on a vision he received many years ago.

Dave was recently honoured at the 2010 International Indigenous Leadership Gathering, received a National Aboriginal Achievement Award and the Volunteer Manitoba Award for Outstanding Community Leadership (2012). In 2011 Dave shared the stage twice with the Dalai Lama in New Jersey and Monterrey, Mexico, to share a message of peace. Recently he has initiated International Roundtables Supporting Ancient Indigenous Knowledge, co-led by US Congressman Dennis Kucinich, and the annual Makoose Ka Win and Vision Quest rites of passage for youth.

William Easter is a Swampy Cree Elder from the Chemawawin First Nation.

Robert Charles Greene was born and raised on reserve in Iskatezaagegan No 39 IFN, where he is a recognized Elder of the Anishnabe Nation.

He attended and survived Cecilia Jeffrey Residential School and graduated with honours from Beaver Brae High School in Kenora, Ontario. Elder Greene has been employed as an Elder at the Selkirk Mental Health Centre and Ochi-Chak-Ko-Sipi Healing Lodge in Crane River First Nation.

D'Arcy Linklater was born in Nisichawayasihk (Nelson House) and raised by his grandparents who taught him to live openly like the water and the river to experience life to the fullest. His great grandfather, Chief Pierre Moose, made the Adhesion to #5 Treaty with the Crown in 1908.

D'Arcy has worked as a trapper, fisherman, hunter and miner. He has been executive director and an elected leader for his Cree Nation for over fifteen years.

Henry Skywater is an Elder of the Dakota Nation, from Birdtail Sioux First Nation.

His grandfather was his role model who introduced him to the traditional way of life, showing him "our way," as he "had it in his heart". Henry gives credit to the influence of many Elders in his life even when he was young and did not see the significance they have in people's lives.

Henry appreciates the importance of "Sun Dancing and Sweat Lodges." Henry is very pleased that our people are beginning to use our history, traditional ways and teachings. "A very positive move," he has a vision that it will continue in our communities and homes.

ABOUT THE ILLUSTRATOR

Henry Guimond is an artist born and raised on the Sagkeeng First Nation, Manitoba, Canada. His artwork is found in many homes and businesses in the community. He has a special talent for painting traditional names.

Henry Guimond is also an architect and builder. He was the architect and head man in the construction of the Turtle Lodge in Sagkeeng First Nation, and is also responsible for the construction of many other beautiful lodges and structures. Henry Guimond does artwork upon request, and can be contacted at turtlelodge@mts.net.

www.theturtlelodge.org
Contact: turtlelodge@mts.net

CPSIA information can be obtained
at www.ICGtesting.com
Printed in the USA
LVHW07n1359030718
582623LV00002B/2/P